DAVID EGGLETON

Published by Otago University Press
Level 1, 398 Cumberland Street
Dunedin, New Zealand
university.press@otago.ac.nz
www.otago.ac.nz/press

First published 2015
Copyright © David Eggleton

The moral rights of the author have been asserted.
ISBN 978-1-877578-93-9

Publisher: Rachel Scott
Editor: Emma Neale
Design/layout: Fiona Moffat

Front cover and internal artwork: Tonu Shane Eggleton
Author photograph: Elizabeth March

Printed in New Zealand by Printlink Ltd, Wellington

THE CONCH TRUMPET

DAVID EGGLETON

OTAGO

CONTENTS

FIRE

NOTES

SHORE

The Conch Trumpet

Stars are setting westward,
other stars are rising eastward:
a handful of sparks on the horizon,
glow-worms on the roof of a cave.
Scorched grains of colour mask
the reasoning power of the human swarm.
Apparitions in mist, cloaked
or vanished, gone to earth,
emerge in the green heart,
the green lungs of divers.
The blueness of the tongue swells.
The sea chest thumps.
The waka is pelted by ochre dust,
by red pōhutukawa, carried in a waterspout.
A centipede paddles.
Squid wreathe miles of black ink;
scuds of smutty carbon drift.
An iron-sand glaze
is fired by a burning forest.
A hand coils pregnant clay.
Neutrinos pinwheel and oscillate through everything.

Ode to the Beach-Wrecked Petrel

Claws grip in gnarled rookeries.
I am brother to tuatara,
a companion to ruru.
I see a kārearea rising at russet dawn
and applaud; I draw breath
at bees in yellow forest:
at bark syrups nuzzled
between black chasms of sea
and white chasms of mountain;
at the glacier's goofy foot blue with cold
that slides over rocks, surfing on;
at those bevies of alpine beauties,
shimmery in sunlight with a forbidding air;
at bladdery kelp, bright green as gherkins,
cast up from under brine, bursting with salt;
and at a petrel,
getting the red carpet treatment
from fallen stamens,
under twisting rātā boughs.

Whakapapa of Rangi the Melody-Maker

Rangi, atua, kūmara, cave spiral,
sizzling mānuka soot and weka fat,
embryo whose tongue protrudes purple.

Karanga wails mingle with drizzle,
curling surf like toetoe flicking water,
and mauri is dancing in the blood.

Hinepūtehue embraces Tāwhirimātea,
maker of storms, with her calm gourd
music, so the grey sky gently weeps.

A pūtōrino chrysalis sings to katydids,
Uenuku casts rainbows for kōkopu,
a ponga forest scars with flame's moko.

A hawk tumbles through a helix of light,
but the legless lizard waits under schist,
beneath mountains' plumed albatross wings.

Rangi, uplifted, wearing a mist mantle,
floats on bier, on waka, on mana reo,
to music sweet as marrow from bone.

Sunday's Song

A tin kettle whistles to the ranges;
dry stalks rustle in quiet field prayer;
bracken spores seed dusk's brown study;
the river pinwheels over its boulders;
stove twigs crackle and race to blaze;
the flame of leaves curls up trembling.
Church bells clang, and sea foam frays;
there's distant stammers of revving engines,
a procession of cars throaty in a cutting,
melody soughing in the windbreak trees,
sheep wandering tracks, bleating alone.
Sunday sings for the soft summer tar;
sings for camellias, fullness of grapes;
sings for geometries of farming fence lines;
sings for the dead in monumental stone;
sings for cloud kites reddened by dusk —
and evening's a hymn, sweet as, sweet as,
carrying its song to streets and suburbs,
carrying its song to pebbles and hay bales,
carrying its song to crushed metal, smashed glass,
and fading in echoes of the old folks' choir.

Trails above Cook Strait

So Farewell Spit, they mocked the seasick;
Tangaroa always gets burnt by the sun.
Bird cries carried by a squall's lick
echo in the ears of Captain Cook,
sunk like an anchor as fathoms break.

Waka creep past wooden islands outrun.
Fish-headed waves snare, skein by skein,
the filigrees of slithery reflection.
Cut those ropes, they said, so the sails can
gather to slowly skywards their way take.

Winged flotillas fly, radiant with lyricism.
Spanked canvas shines in accumulation,
buoyed up by air like honeycombs of foam.
Waves dance in perpetual motion,
stitching the Tasman under swell of moon.

Raukura

Stone clacks on stone,
so creek lizards slither,
runnels slip through claws,
each cloud's a silver feather.
Mountains flex then soar;
the red tussock pulses.
River's mouth is drowned,
when ocean surges, green
below dark vaulted forest.
The salt spray mist, violet,
granular as dust, climbs
to grasp snow mountains
in fog layers, and above
glides the boat of the moon.

The Hook of Maui

A fanged shank yanks him from open sea.
Silken jellyfish glisten on hot iron-sand.
Mottled green light tattoos a drug-blue gaze.
Stingrays undulate along sunlit nerves.
The road snakes, and cars fishtail in gravel.
His ears are earthenware, glazed by mud.
Gold toetoe rise in hair-triggers from his armpits.
His filaments snarl round a plastic comb.
Police bolt-cutters snag on his tongue stud.
His lungs are stopped with red scoria splinters.
His lips turn black from a summit's pure snows.
His blanket's unbound clay, slid from bedrock.
Night's moths flutter from the cave of his mouth.
He dreams he's woken, wrapped in calm water.

Hei-tiki

Spindle-shank birds step on shadows;
estuary's sheen dances the tidelines.
Mānuka buds into a white floor of stars,
and summer's kihikihi husks shrivel.
Sheep nuzzle hollows of particular hills;
froth billows and eddies on farm streams.
A paddock of thistles anchors the view;
all God's azure peels to an apricot blaze.
Dark water funnels a reservoir's turn
from spider colonies and cocoon trails.
Cobweb fleeces, hung by spinners in orbs,
glow like ghosts, like ship's rigging.
The tuatara's eye beholds the moon's eye.
A stone hei-tiki is dug out of the earth
by a settler grubbing the first garden.
Hatchlings glow and struggle from nets.
A poled kauri scow floats off the bar.
In this swamp, only buzzing of fat
horse-flies over a long drop, but heat's
sump soakage stews up tannins,
the dappled tarn is frog-eyed with shine,
and beeswax softens. Under the sun,
the shed at the end of the road warps.

Lighting Up in a Singer Vogue

Winter tilting on the beach groans,
and daylight's embers are buried.
A mechanical digger gouges clay
for a trench to pipe the seagull's cry.
Swept by breezes, the soul rolls thin.
Surf streamers flex their vortex crests
under skies whiter than albatross wings
launched for horizon's arc of ocean.
Mist is flying, in pages torn from books.
Slid beneath a sparse quilt of snow,
the land's skeleton reaches to hug you.

Trampers in Westland

I
Acrobatic sandflies,
    Satan's fiends,
their powers and dominions
tumbling clouds driven by
         frenzied bloodlust;
living mobiles,
    demonstrating dark energies
of sub-atomic particles;
we walk
    in secret peoplehood
through these cross-questioning
    insect swarms.

II
We molluscs expand,
    by an ebbing tide,
         dripping;
we beached seals,
    sand-encrusted ones,
        our red-rimmed eyes
mournfully raised
    to the overcast skies;
with long wet hair,
    trailing seaweed,
        the puddle dripped into,
rising round our knees.

III
Solitaries
    in alert reverie,
        listening to shush, shush,
rhymes of the sea;
    feathery smears up arms,
        feet mottled salt-and-pepper,
soggy-bottomed swim-togs,
    or bikinis towel-wrapped;
perched on odd driftwood forms
    by bonfire's crackle and woosh,
omnipresent dark hills,
    morepork! cry from the bush.

Fiord Haka

Rūaumoko slaps thighs, thumps
torso, and groans heavily,
busting moves to rattle gravity:
needle-scratches a seismograph,
making dolphins leap for the starry.
Our echoing ship rumbles, bumps,
and the fiord wobbles up from sleep,
whaleback thrashing around midnight,
before gurgling back down to slumber,
between rockfall splashing hemmed.
By day's steepled buttresses we tramp,
next to river's muscle-tug flow west,
rain a velvet-nosed champagne wetness —
such fine balances of skimmed rainfall,
such varieties of mould and mosses,
on pathway's crumbled clay crust
a dolphining fern curve, a feather flutter;
while in haphazard winks and touches
broken sunlight brightens the gemmed
webbings of branches, water's drift:
all misty impediments to a clarity
difficult to determine in unsettlement.

Moriori Dendroglyphs

green tongues lollop round branches
through wounds in bark with deep
affliction like tattoos freshly fingered

surf's blind gravel spat from the sea
rain streaking a small plane's windscreen
as it lands on wind-flattened paddock

black waves of coal an ancient tide
clenched between clay layers
and just them walking in ideation

on limestone walls under kite claws

INLAND

Syzygy

Moon dreams of moonlight,
cracking sutures of the skull open.
Mouth, moth, o moonlight, flicker.
Dance, moons of May.
Dance, moons of torch-shine.
Moon, tossed over our heads, a ball,
sails towards the net.
Scry the moon, note down marks you see
on her surface reflected in still water.
Moon, round mirror,
veined solid slub, a prism.
A telescope, gibbous grim-moon,
a drinkers' moon — full, fat, cheerfully bright.
Melon moon, pregnant to many moons.
Moon conjuring mystic syzygy,
with the sun in harmony.
Moon's spectral lake, draped weightless
with moonlight, gathering shadow.
Tarot moon, shuffling decks of the zodiac,
leaving runnels of shadow across her forehead.
Knight errant, his black pennant flags hung
on a Golden Holden out in the scrub,
with mattock, shovel and a body,
leaning on the bonnet,
ponders the mellow moon hugely aloft
and crossed by tatters of cloud,
its insignia a kind of stigma.
Moon, her abdomen girdled with stars,
she carries the teardrop of sorrow
tattooed on her cheek.
All the phantom pregnancies sigh and cry.

Once in a blue moon,
everyone grows older, if you need something
to cry on, here's my shoulder,
not cold, but nor does it smoulder.
Hey you, this is the room to chill in,
with its moony glow
of black and blue.
Moon? City lights swallow it,
but there's the neon moon,
and the sizzle of its brand burns till dawn.

Roadkill

fleece fur feather
petrol fumes
hard rubber wheels
and leather

Bounty

Years stack up
like hymn books;
days run like rabbits,
or writhe in talons.

Soft breeze ruffles trees;
a hand reaches
into a hatful
of raffle tickets.

Hydrangeas, too,
sport bitter blooms
still sunlit within rain's
green abyss.

From trance of rubies,
gold, emeralds,
time's buzz wakes you
to zebra stripes.

Pull the catch —
it remains in light;
but burning whale oil
blackens the moon.

Hawk and Butterfly

As the kāhu, a hairline, coasts in clear blue,
yellow gorse stretches under big rock's face,
and barbed wire's strung, enclosing our place.
So we pace at the gates of Te Papa,
made a paradise from haka to haka,
for kiwi by kiwi just passing through,
each carrying a piece of thin silver fern,
cut while you wait from corrugated tin.
Billy's boiling away, down back of beyond;
planed kauri frames a fret-sawn view.
We're listening to the rugby in lemon light,
with a longing for victory, with a dog's sigh.
Rain flutters from horses, skips off a frond,
and forms a sheen on roads in the wet;
till the sun comes out to weakly, and yet
steadily, illuminate the monarch butterfly.

Minute Bodies Falling

Dawn hung on the horizon,
vistas of unending south,
skinny land between,
green ribbons rising, falling,
kilometre after kilometre,
and minute bodies falling,
tiny lives in cobs, hives or nests,
enmeshed, knitted, buckled,
midge, beetle, dragonfly aflitter,
swarms intricate above a river —
all hesitations swept away,
barbered siftings falling in place,
floss, fleece, feather —
a scrap become airborne, trembly,
as pelt or hoof or eye might be,
as fabric in turbulence, skimpy —
the whispered caress of wind-chill,
near sheer, on the move, balanced
uneasily, piecing together,
flake by flake in surface tension,
gauze wrap, ivory drape,
bony frame, enshadowed hill,
ridge-top's face of thunder,
gunmetal, frost, silver,
staunch, blackened, clattery —
the gale grown, bruised and bled,
to bared teeth, evening fur,
contour after contour,
sleet working a white comb,
weight of clouds raked and torn,
streaks haphazard tumbled,

over patchwork jerseys of farms,
enmeshed, knitted, buckled,
province woven to province,
in weathered solitude
of roads, lights, transmission —
staccato of hail's confetti
on untidy bush from sky dishevelled,
outlandish perspectives sunk low,
in dirt seams, in leaf-scissored,
peekaboo flyaways overturned,
to turn and turn as ice,
as minute bodies
that parachute to peaks —
vistas of unending south,
caked with snow at dawn.

Summer Rain

Spring trees grow collections of wands,
to conjure gently the colour green,
but in summer drum-taps bounce on water
to ease a tension of the skin,
and when summer rain thunders,
then starts to dance, it is itself the romance,
prancing down the street with silvery feet,
kicking a frou-frou cancan from verandah overhang,
splashing the spatterdashes of an entrance.

Rain brings Fred Astaire's tap-tap across the roof,
before a razz of jazz is given tumultuous applause,
the ozone in the air extinguished like snuff
of golden beeswax melted in candles.
Petulant petals quiver in crimson.
Rain bodies forth a spectacular
earthworm welcome from hitherto undistinguished lawn.

After the storm's glance moves on,
silence fills with bird song, the sheen of datura,
sky-blue of the violet, whiteness of carnation,
scarlet glow of iceland poppies —
until the very nectarines blush, as teeth break skin,
grass dries out, heat splits pods,
and all summer breathes from the garden.

Hydrangeas

Shrubbery's floral bells.
Delicate as grace-notes, tough as wicker-knots.
Gathered to empurpled perms.
Arrayed like Parfait Amour liqueur shots.
Petalled bathing caps
of a legion of synchronised swimmers,
blue in a hubbub.
The charge of the light opera brigade
towards the best seats,
clustered as a violet rinse contagion.
Floating tethers of balloons in delicate pinks.
Sleepy heads of nursery beds,
cobwebbed in leafy dreams.
Powdered wigs of toffs and swells,
who lord it over a fancy-dress carnival at dusk.
Hazy as clapped chalk dusters
in school monitor's grip.
Bubbly as champagne, snipped
and mounted in vases on ledges.
A bobble of tennis-court fans,
applauding their own cornucopia
to garden's very echo of umpire calls.
Pom-pom girls, cheerleaders
of suburban rah-rah squads.
Amid stridulations of summer days,
of lark-soaring trills and cheep-cheeps,
hydra-headed and growing more heads,
crouched under masses of cumulus,
colours are your confabulations,
and flowering in that assumption,
you are the crest of the wave.

On Recrudescence of Waterfalls After All-Night Rain

Before the movies they had waterfalls:
movement spectacular, streamed from bluffs;
gorgeous reels, unspooled in wedding-dress train;
blessings and curses that coterminously reign.
A heart surge, over stone, all spray and rivulets;
spangled dribble of some open-mouthed
giant, deaf-making, whose tresses spill,
wig upon wig, to gravel mosaics
between clay gullies, where the kinetic pool
of its massed body weaves and ripples.
So strewn, grappling gravity, it headlong flings
between ridge arms, to the blow-hole
of a reptile fossil look-out, wet with glitter
mined as popcorn additive for *Lord of the Rings*.

Catchment

Trees heave, flap, grizzle,
as wind croons rock-a-bye,
but roots grapple beneath
hill crests that jag and scoop
at squalls groaning like bullocks
hauling trunks across ponga banners,
bracken skirts, tumbled bird balconies,
in genesis of rain spawning
on creeks gurgling through gullies,
while drizzle's spit settles as mist
which swirls cool bulk over paspalum,
and a weatherboard church's drummed roof.
White silks sag to shroud macrocarpas.
From slicked fronds erratic tick-tocks
tell time to crumpled rock slides,
and uprisings of moisture crawl into pines
to breathe vapour and breed in darkness.
Water wrangles and spouts below
boulders, clambers and deepens.
It sings, and glides its fingers
out of ponds sewn with green seams.
More water pulses and slithers
from bogs, flicks silver along traceries
of gravel, and spools over mud-banks,
punching loose humpty-dumpty clods,
until with a rush the weight of river
hurls its roar higher than a rainbow.

Aniwaniwa

Trembling across sky's cream-dress train
appears the arc of rainbow's membrane,
sun's burst-through flame
kindles colour from overcast;
a hawk shifts back to the river,
where a hillside has slid down a gorge
as the river scrubs round it with a surge,
in mocking glub-glub cataract past
a wet-gold bloom of gorse and broom,
half-echoed by bellbird's syrupy call,
beyond clumped kidney ferns, slick
in iridescence from the late squall;
while on dark earth's mudcake,
toy-like, a yellow bulldozer squats,
by rimu pit-sawn weatherboards stacked
inside a tin shed camouflaged with rust;
the greasy teeth of a chainsaw
also there, trickled with orange sawdust,
and all around a panorama
of muscular, jostling hills,
under the authority of upthrust crags,
draped with pine forest
as the switchback road twitches
on hairpins for a timber treatment plant;
and the flare of the sun
is on the river slanted in its chasm,
as if probing for incandescence,
as flow half back-turns, then forward gleams,
ripples like numerals of surplus rolling coastwards
and is squizzed at by satellite lenses,
a rivering witness-ribbon of currency,

rubbing elbows with pulp and paper,
toothpicks and matchwood;
so night engulfs each good pozzie,
beneath pinched heaven's pot of gold,
and bird chorus extinguished.

Hokitika

We skipped the town, but stopped
in a picnic area to gaze at wetland
lit by spontaneous combustion
of the sun and trickling like armpits
as gnats swarmed from hell's waiting room,
the open air a decompression chamber,
after a long drive down the coast's curls
of fern and surf done by a copperplate hand.
Trees punched holes in the sky, like ground-to-air missiles.
Weka eyed us, and pecked the bejesus out of snail shells.
Stone tablets beneath the river's flow
laid out an unreadable mosaic of bushlore;
a faded DOC sign wrote its message
to posterity; and spidery signature
tunes of motor engines signed the mist,
then faded down the road.
The wood-hens scurried under the table,
as we shredded cold chicken, unscrewed the thermos,
shrugged at drizzle's worthless
banknotes of forest leaves,
damp cigars of twigs,
and sucked against tarry teeth
scalding tea, hot as tears.
In a map the size of a handkerchief,
I wrapped a wishbone,
and placed it in the waste-bin —
all this stored in motion capture of memories,
like bread crumbs carried off by birds of the mind.

Nor'wester Flying

Gorse-cutters know they are quids in;
river's pledge is so polished it shines,
as a blind wind gropes the sand dunes.

Cloud whispers brush daylight's ear;
fern question-marks form a bush encore;
forlorn heat swings cobbed in webs.

Stone outcrops sideways knock the gale;
grasshoppers thread leaf-storm's blade,
paddocks kick for touch on the tar-seal.

Cries of birds interrogate bareback hills
that reveal bleached treatment for bones;
river's harp pings; and music of twig-falls
is blown away by thunder's aerodrome.

Observatory

Drams of dew shove stars out at dawn.
Dreams of wilding pines stalk tussock fog.
Mountain gowns in pristine satin fold
alcove upon alcove away, to await storms.
Creek music mutters from fiddlehead ferns.
Bees zap lupins; glacier grins at glacier.
Scrubbed-clean scenery hangs its calendar
of lakes at a point in space
where sky's blue crush begins.
The stone sails beneath the sun.

Desirous of mud, of sacks of spuds,
of cows in ranging crowds,
and uncoffined by tumbled outcrops,
earth rises from the roll of scree slopes,
hauls through dry bush in stillness,
feels dusty tyres in revolution,
their makeshift patterns over distance,
then runs on under falling night, satellites,
moons of Saturn seen through a telescope,
dark's singular tumulus of Mount John.

River

Begin, spring,
on steep range.
Unfurl fern-scroll,
in light sing,
glance off things,
shimmer by swimmers,
swirl green as willows
stirring tips in summer;
surface under bridges,
while land turns,
to autumn,
where leaves freckle,
winds raise chaff,
dust braids thorns,
hawks hollow the sky,
and warmth creeps
from currents, open
slather for winter
ocean
ever-closer.

WAITAHA

Alpenglow Reddening

White meteor's tail flashes across the stars,
then a red meteor's,
then sparks fly down the Main Divide,
as sun rays climb —
over jutting crags, sub-alpine basins,
montane prairies, dry foothills,
balconies of stone in back-country nests,
swamp cushions gemmed with dew,
green oils and buttery lights of the plains;

over common weal of riven rock,
over broken scarps of clay,
over glacier histories carving the land,
over rubbled cloud piling high —
yet the tuatara of time barely shifts ground.

Orogenesis

Dug from tiny earth gestures, sometimes a convulsion,
shale fans on the move thaw and freeze: hot then cold.
Frost-heave lifts flakes of rock: ice melts; soil slumps.
Sensors might catch quakes low on the Richter scale
that throw everything up as if off big bull shoulders.
Delicately dancing greywacke seams on tip-toe
contract and flex. Crumbly, bald, boundless strata
bunch and flank, make a pressure graph of fault lines:
axis squeezed between the dialectic of sun and rain.

Some force has left no stone unturned but tumbles
— down climactic slopes steep as speedy escalators —
each to seek true weight on a trial and error basis,
till, caught by river rapids, they bank up as shingle,
and, an eternity later, riverbed dust blown sky-high.

Cloud-Piercer

… a great land uplifted high …

———ABEL TASMAN

I
On winter's serrated edge glints
snow's teeth, talons, feather-slick tints.

Nothing loath, prowled by air's current,
great alps bulk above canopy.

Below zero, lofted mist tufts
become crystal slush in winds rough.

Gliding plumaged ice is blown back;
rock ribs are hammered by storm's wrack.

Gangs of gales through lone ravines roar;
ride the trough to its blizzard core.

II
Amid glazed buttercup summers
graze short-horned flightless grasshoppers,

while carnivorous sundews wink
from black bogs as hapless bugs sink.

Black-backed cicadas bask in shine;
bat-winged flies, likewise heated, whine.

Mountain weta's jelly-green blood
never freezes — these giants brood.

Spiders, lacewings, and the stunner:
god of ugly creatures — Wetaponga.

Wilderness

The early writers echoed one another
to haul narratives of settlement into being,
as if cramming more sail on good ship *Rhapsody*.
'Mount Cook, greenstone country, middle island',
was 'stupendous', 'precipitous', 'gigantic' —
the sublime defined by extremes: peaks, troughs,
breathtaking gulfs, gulps of cold illumination.
They had journeyed to another planet, unholy
place of savages, a nameless nothingness,
rising up from whaling anchorages, a frontier,
a found blank wasteland they would remake;
colonial cartographers with plans for panoramas,
assembled from myths, memories and obsessions.
Surveyors' pegs put land-rush fever on the map:
a cathedral town, nostalgia for a new pastoral,
harmonious balance and flourishing civilisation
drawn from mire and slime, fire and flood,
Bible's promise of spacious and fertile plains,
the mountainous banner of the Church of England.
So wilderness fearful rang with place names,
possessive metaphors, legal claims, picnic idylls,
landmarks staked by Charles Torlesse or Thomas Cass,
Charlotte Godley, Lady Barker, the nowhere of Erewhon.
Thus Samuel Butler looked up to stony limits,
went searching for paydirt in magnetic ore:
'At every shingle bed we came to … we lay down
and gazed into the pebbles with all our eyes.'

Place and Mana

But nowhere shared borders with somewhere:
Cook called it *Tovypoenammu*, also known as
Te Waka a Maui, the mighty rowboat of Maui,
proving a palimpsest: land already named.
Governor Hobson declared it *terra nullius*,
while Henry Kemp bought 'nowhere' — with coins, threats —
from Kāi Tahu, who staged passive resistance;
land did, too, with tremors, floods, winds, dust storms.
Tāwhirimātea — god of turbulent weather — raged,
as features were titled after Greek gods, Christ's churchmen,
and 'the Canterbury block' broken up like chocolate.
Rivers lashed their tails to find their wairua Anglified —
Rakahuri became 'Ashley', Waimakariri 'Courtney',
Rakaia 'Cholmondeley', Hakatere 'the Ashburton',
Rangitata 'the Alford' — so the big powerful ones
rose up, drowned many, took back their names.

Omarama: Place of Moonlight

Moa, that stalking angel, conjures up a wing;
plucks a feather; begins to tattoo with soot and oil.

Bees journey across charcoal-drawn country;
gold pollen flares in black beech forest.

Moths burn their secret dyes onto raupō kites;
and ochre pigment nets the soaring pouākai.

A tohunga wanders the whenua remembered,
where moonlit basalt heads wailed prophecies.

As lakes blue the skies with their glacier melt,
limestone's grain's rubbed back to scratch again.

Time-lapsed maps, seen by glow-worm gleams
in a burial cave under a hill, fade in bright sun.

The Granary

… our ship her path is cleaving
The flashing waters through …
— JAMES EDWARD FITZGERALD

Dolphins rode the bows' slather coastwards;
spars reefed canvas like coiling shrouds
of foam children's hands clutched at and lost
in the frenzy of arrival at Port Lyttelton,
the journey to the junction of bridle tracks,
where Christchurch sprouted from raupō marsh:
place of pre-Adamites, and of pilgrims brought
by the First Four Ships and Wakefield's vision,
written of in dairies, letters, novels, memoirs.
Seven kingfishers on a yardarm watched moths
jotter out of night's inkwell to brush a lantern.
At Kaiapoi stockade pou made pāua eyes
at what was fenced in and what was fenced out.
Boundary posts followed single furrows ploughed
as markers for cart tracks joined by ferry punts.
Bullocks dragged drays laden with migrant luggage
towards the interior; brought back bales of flax.
Axles and axes led to wheat and sheep, level roads.
Stark shanty towns settled into golden tussock;
gravels were panned for colours through a sluice box.
The plains ended sliced, diced and gridlocked
by shagroons, cockatoos, gentry, merchants.
Then railways: Te Kooti called trains Whistling God
of the Pākehā. They carried heavyweight ploughs
to grub out deep-rooting cover. Oats, barley went in,
and thirty varieties of oak tree, lawns for croquet —
tōtara stumps removed with jacks and shovels;

the iron bars beaten into patu for rangatira rusted.
Bush felled, ryegrass seasoned with white clover
was broadcast across fields, and livestock grazed.
The chequerboard grew; followed roads up-country,
under clamp of the southerly buster, the arch
of nor'west cloud hovering above the Main Divide,
above dotted dairy herds, moving carpets of wool,
above lamb and flag and wheatsheaf shields,
barbed-wire symphonies, songs of district and parish,
strung-out telegraph, aeroplane's first manned flight.

The Burnt Text of Banks Peninsula

All over Banks Peninsula in the middle of the nineteenth century,
sure-footed on slopes, forest shook out wings;
could not flee; began to singe:
the white cloak was not feathers but smoke —
a hīnaki of creeks twisted and broke.
Axes more weighty than an adze split bark;
tackles harnessed to bullocks dragged logs apart;
peat exposed beneath fallen kahikatea began to rot.
Steam sawmills chugged to life; wairua shrank away:
great trunks of tōtara wallowed down gullies,
stumped up to blades spinning in light and shade,
were cradled so the timber sawn would not warp —
wanted for floors, walls, bridges and wharves.
Wreathes of flames combed gullies to char strewings
and bare blunt brute land: its broken-off stands
reduced to shadows, scars, and a few nīkau palms —
the gallows haze of carbonised trees, intended to purify
and fertilise, hung over paddocks until Gallipoli.

Off the Sheep's Back

Sheep like maggots on a rabbit's tawny pelt …
—— BASIL DOWLING

Sheep crawl on the hill's broad back like swollen slaters under the stone of the sky …
—— PATRICIA GLENSOR

I watch the sheep like a pestilence
Pouring over the slopes …
—— DENIS GLOVER

Each a crest, each a herald, each emblazoned,
countless on the coat of arms of Victoria's island,
obedient to the virtue of Meekness, hooves on her lap;
the land's black pennant snapping in fierce loyalty:
Meekness, Fidelity, Moderation, then Prosperity.

Tossed-curl cloud: classers fleece cloud that bigs
itself up as sunset in full array — like sewn sacks
stacked to climb for glory in wool stores — or those
risen barred streaks that drift silken, as flocks
crown summits like shocks of snow to the stars.

The fickle trade fair of rag trade's latest collections,
wisps and still more wisps, clipped scanty at first;
not skimped on, skerricks wound-in off jumped-up
merinos: pelt with a heartbeat to snag rosettes and thorns,
before a steel talon rips open the chosen bale of product.

In dustbowl cemeteries of flyblown carcass paddocks,
skeleton thistles and the rabbits' gibbet wire fence,
everything that stinks is holy; Bible's seven-year drought

wavering through bubbled glass of farmhouse windows:
rusted bouquets of ironmongery, car hulks overgrown.

Picturesque classics of ruination, unsettlement,
a Budget black as burnt stubble on a Canterbury run,
black as coal in rail wagons rumbling to Lyttelton;
then a day when shepherds survey the blue horizon
like Prince Aragon: from the peak of a wool-boom.

Rakaia

Dark feather of the rainbird, riroriro,
sweeps over the ranges, bringing watercolours,
as the facets of ridges ripple with snow-melt,
and each angled rock-face spawns waterfalls,
clear threads woven to join the heart of water
beating in a youthful stampede of spring creeks
that pull apart to bolt through bush; so spiral,
purl, englobe boulders, and jostle back together,
forming a restless racing torrent that collects
brisk water, slow water, slack water, twirligig pools,
ravelling these ribbons and vines into a river strand
descending the mighty spine of the Southern Alps;
and gathering in the flurries of many tributaries,
until the Rakaia springs out of the mountains,
a wily and seasoned campaigner meandering
in lacy loops and twirls through channels,
the gravity of gravels a growl in river's throat:
Rakaia, visible portion of a continuous seepage
pulsing subterranean to the sea, flicking braids,
the gliding pulse of its groundwater going strong.

Haast Amongst the Moa

Mountains are your eagle claws,
your aquiline beak.
Maverick feathery prey in tussock,
swamp or sandhill,
they were dug from a bog.
Now home is a hollow log
in a museum diorama,
while the billy boils.
The taxidermied crowd regards you
with glass eyes.
Muscular Christians,
whole mustering gangs,
have gone the way of all flesh.
A kea's scream rattles down scree
and up hawk spurs;
a greenstone mere thrills to the marrow.
Wrestling with a taniwha,
on a turbulent riverbed;
eels of water welling from a bore,
as rātā bloom maps the province in red.

Resurrection of the Waimakariri Floodplain

*A four per cent risk exists in any one year that water will break out
onto the floodplain.*

— THE PRESS, 14 FEBRUARY 2009

The green ark's greyed-out by rain,
as shadow-lines of solitude softly
follow clouds' prowling pillars,
wade shallows dragged from marrow,
getting mud between prim suburbs,
where waters overturn the rituals
by which on earth we gain traction.

Rain is a soakage that brims swamps;
background lurching up to take over;
cloudage scoured out of farm tanks;
phantasm to erode transmission pylons,
nebulous, amphibious, mysterious.
Further back, snow cauldrons swirl,
and hydro-lakes begin to swell.

Fiddle-coils of catchments re-tune;
storm bursts splash against window glass,
like fume of pinot gris noisily decanted;
and small towns rediscover lost culverts.
Straddling swing bridges are diamonded.
Though fretting gardens tap with tears,
bush-clad declivities exult with wetness.

Headlands are prows turned to the waves;
water scrawls on fish-scaled fence netting,
takes the shape of wind, the shape of inland,

to colour all the golds, reds, blues, silvers
of tussock on flanks of the high country;
revive the eels, the mudfish, the īnanga,
kōaro, kōkopu, watchful waterfowl.
And there, oilskin-clad and squinting,
the Waimak thumps against its stopbanks,
feeling the weight of an ancient history.

Mystic Courses of Camper Vans

The mystic courses of camper vans might follow
the three great passes — Arthur's, Lewis, Burke's —
that lead a jig through dizzy Canterbury,
as helicopters might muster the trek of weather,
chop-chop-chop of an air ambulance, or rich
tourist anglers chasing brown trout deep inland.

The mystic courses of camper vans might follow
memories of roads, long, shingled and dusty,
to where the flat begins to crumple to foothills,
before the mountains swell all compasses west,
as railway lines once stitched seams of the quilt
on slow ascent past horse paddocks, church bells.

The mystic courses of camper vans might follow
heat shimmers over a tarsealed melting highway
that's flung out black like a bullocky's whip,
into broom and lupin murmuring with bees,
hawk rising blood-beaked and mottled for open sky,
distant mares' tails looping ahead of a storm.

The mystic courses of camper vans might follow
bird snares of Tāne-mahuta, and find kea
on the spree, skirling with glee on updraughts,
might find river-bird nests wrybill plovers flee,
and strutting pūkeko in cloud-cuckoo heaven,
as lizards furl tongues by forks of Rangitata.

The mystic courses of camper vans might follow
the sunshower twinkling away over a hill
to a wire-strainer twang and banjo shovel clang,

creeks like stewed tannins from tumbled tea urns,
a white cascade falling in smoking arrows,
whale paths beneath Tangaroa's salt-soaked surge.

The mystic courses of camper vans might follow
a magnetic bone needle pointing out the path
of the green fish Poutini, who hid in the Arahura
as wet greenstone glazed with rainbow haze;
then found by Waitaha was carried to Kaiapoi,
so making the whole island Te Wai Pounamu.

Old Man Nor'wester

Sometimes Old Man Nor'wester blows, and so exhumes,
amid dust moving, shingle skating, braids shifting,
the rainshadow shape of sheep rustler James McKenzie,
who strolled, dead broke and crook to boot, only to fluke
a landscape he wrapped up tight and carried like a swag,
taking seven-league strides across the Mackenzie Country,
preaching sermons in Gaelic to his dog as skinks lay hidden
like shrunken dragons among rocks of subalpine basins
furrowed back to basics by that wind; tufts of wool
chasing across the barrel-vault-blue vastness of the sky.

McKenzie, though, vanished beyond lost cairn markers
long ago, his straggly beard legacy of wilding pines,
ragwort, Yorkshire fog, yarrow, gorse, king devil,
mouse-eared hawkweed, a rogues' gallery gathering
in our sanctum sanctorum of ancient lakes and rivers
we will not sandblast back to the past; as powerlines
sough, and scullers row for New Zealand against drag
on Ruataniwha; and rabbits start from bootfalls
in this mirrorland of desires rustled for subdivisions,
hydro-electric dams, boating, the remains of film sets.

Dragonfly wheel energies of Lakes Tekapo, Pukaki,
Ohau, the colour of ground-down pounamu, spin
into the Waitaki, as Old Man Nor'wester skips
dynamic water, flicks it over, rippling sunshine's
dismantle of ice into scalding light; until the light
darkens, pent-up, or sings seawards, past folded
hills seamed with gullies, farmers' corrugated faces,
electricity snaking north and south, the fizz of life;
and then in the night those gusts trying to prise open
a greenstone door slammed tight on the underworld.

The Motherlode

We put on our identities as consumers to enter Enzed's dairy kingdom,
with its casino trickle of coins.
We put on our identities as citizens to debate the moral absolute
of water, the commons where the water is.
Sixty per cent of all water used in the nation is used in Canterbury,
and much of it for irrigation.
So here come the corporations, the speculators, the anonymous
investors to join the primary producers
converted to the conversion of farms to dairying land,
as if the dairy milk bubble might always expand,
and water be abstracted so that milk goes on sloshing into vats
in a glorious hundred-year plan.

Where thousands of moa once stalked, cows now move to stand,
big bladders on legs, bagpipes of udders in sway.
Out they come, crowding onto the paddock at more than two grand
a pop, dozens then hundreds, then by the thousand.
Impregnated by machine, to be milked by machine in a brown land
turned green by machine: great cranes that rotate their way,
as wingbeats of water flutter and flash, pumped from sand
and silt and gravel seepage deep down into the light of day.
Canted metal gantries that gush their plumes toward the snow
make out of a dustbowl lush lawns for herds to graze,
and just such fecund possibility of milkflow makes eyes glow,
brings shiny grilles of tankers barrelling through the heat haze.

So watch the procession pass heavy with milk to the shed.
Beast hooves plug cropped grass in mud-rhythms,
and bones jut through strained skins of a commodity measured
in billions, jaws working cud, and soft muzzles lathered.
Gargoyles of the Plains, when, through drains, their muck is hosed:

ammonia nitrates into canals, ditches, rivers degraded.
Clear-running streams, wetlands of yesteryear, redesigned
by the centre-pivot irrigators' stuttering yield,
as alien, post-industrial, futuristic, damaged, starved,
over-abstracted, and with deliberation ruthlessly consumed
for calcium for bone, for powder, for yoghurt fat-reduced:
our milk lakes, beneath mountains buckling on tectonic plates.

Q Feb 22

Clocked at nine to one, the CBD rocked —
then, unchristchurched, jumped and bounced in
the strongest ever recorded up and down quake.
Plasterwork was a child's plate of jelly dropped.
Through fissures wide as a street, spirit figures slipped;
and rivers whipped their gravel braids.
The old raupō swamp sagged like a trampoline.
Asylums crumbled; a time capsule popped.

God's finger moved, and having moved broke off,
to roll away into quicksands of risen silt.
A scattering wall of bricks fell across the sky;
and clay slapped to make a golem shrank away.
A chess knight rode across a fever-white grid.
Keys to the Absolute unlocked doors to a Void.
Earthquakeville was a dungeon, damply out of joint;
all the toads escaped, scattering boulders as they went.

Sinkholes rappelled through geological time;
Four Avenues were a broken Harlequin, nursed by Columbine.
Dust whisked about, like grimy Victorian skirts;
soapbox orators of Cathedral Square fled their desserts.
The Strip stripped down to the Avon; the Avon sailed to sea.
Town bells failed to clang with hour-keeping urgency.
Just below the surface, making the surface ping,
a swamp foetus was fluttering, fluttering like a gauzy wing.

Grounded

In the earthquake season,
the krump.

In the earthquake season,
electro-convulsive nanoseconds tie on a straitjacket.

In the earthquake season,
ogres thump under the floorboards with large staves.

In the earthquake season,
the ground flexes, twitches,
and sometimes levitates like a kung-fu fighter.

In the earthquake season,
a bee burrows into a flower,
and the whole rose bush quivers in the grab of an afternoon
that vibrates like the fell of a dog pelt panting.

In the earthquake season,
thousands of shod feet cross and recross pavements
and crowd above trapdoors that might be under litter,
as mortal tremors skip away like practical jokers.

In the earthquake season,
if push-me pull-you land masses can take an aeon
to travel a stone's throw, then they move in an instant,
move with a kind of peristaltic motion,
to gobble up buildings, tear at lawns,
snag teeth on powerlines and groan with heavy lifting.

In the earthquake season,
a plate spinning on a pole wobbles gently,
the cracked-open night stirs with the smell of caves,
and beneath the puddled muddiness of clouds,
sailing ship masts of kahikatea list and right.
A gecko scuttles from bark of a stoved-in ark.

In the earthquake season,
all the buildings hereabouts tip-toe round in darkness,
bumping into walls of other buildings so lightly,
water barely trembles in a glass, and residents'
sleep patterns remain unbroken.

In the earthquake season,
when ground opens up, it goes back to the beginning.
Over the Garden City, starlight is singing.

EREWHON UNEARTHED

Untold

untold those years that rung as gold
like gold poured out of a crucible
the yellow lure of sky ablaze
cracked clay's cliff-edge crumble
flung dust in a stinging haze
perfume stealing good as gold
the song of lilies lupins sun-showers
gold in kōwhai gorse mānuka
gold of root hairs that climb from mud
gold of fern sap bubbled from ponga
gold underpinnings in a cloud-span
gold's beaten froth that scuds to land
gold bell-chimes of quarter-hours

gold's branch upon branch in rivers
gold in bird feathers mottled salt
gold spills of tobacco leaf makings
gold unreeled and flaked or chipped
gold the twig the nest the thread
gold the stump the nub the chunk
gold the skin the light's gleams pulsing
gold splinters dyes scourings
gold a broken-handled axehead
that only yesterday it seems
split the felled tōtara trunk
for five hundred fenceposts
and an old man's coffin

The Visitation

Mackenzie kneels near Waitaki,
enters a tree poem in a log-book.
Seals it up with highway tar,
hammering leaf against leaf.
Mountains echo his amphitheatre.
Raindrops pluck skins on Pukaki.

Ignoring creek splutter, rain's tangi,
stump by stump arrivals advance
across the Devil's Half-Acres
to massacres of feathery kiwi.
As one of that kidney Hātana knew,
Mackenzie loosens his neck-tie for a dance.

In his gunny sack he clutches harpoon heads,
gathers pounamu blades from iwi.
Lantern flames shadowbox the canvas,
and flittering shoals of galaxiids
fall in stars over whale-boat shapes,
silent waka anchored, silhouetted.

Daybreak the colour of rosehips, Mackenzie
climbs from Rākaihautū's footprint,
clings to bowsprit of the windjammer pitched
on the big top of a spinning nor'wester —
with a spyglass of islands crooked in his arm,
and all the ocean before him.

Rust Casting an Iron Spell

Within a kōwhai grove in spring,
or closed in winter's mist,
chase the grail of the whale,

chase an earthquake swarm,
domino of the avalanche,
revolution the tractors bring.

Hit a slump, close the mill,
unbolt the coal range,
and walk off the farm,

making tracks for town.
Leave the hand-me-downs
among the plum trees still;

chests of tea, a bush brewery,
flax ropes frail on kauri rail,
the phantoms of opium,

gold grave a night hawk saved,
raupō hides where hope abides,
a whole fleet washed to sea,

coffins mashed, rivers slain,
hāngī rocks piled sky-high
and girdled by a rusty chain.

Clocks, Calendars, Nights, Days

Bitterness of bees dying out,
honeyless clouds, forest drought,
lights red, yellow, charcoal's grain,
eyes smarting from a world on fire,
air thick with grit; cleave to it.
    By clocks, calendars, nights, days

Bog-cotton frenzy of winter
dancing erasures over hills,
leaf-litter corrected by snow;
fog quick to swallow the sea,
then starting in on the shore.
    By clocks, calendars, nights, days

Skerricks of twigs skim high,
flung far from grips of fists;
remember to dip your bucket
deep into the morning sun,
but don't drown in apathy.
    By clocks, calendars, nights, days

So down in the earth's mouth,
a slow song about the rain,
as you heave from the dark
to hear a thunderous beat
knocking on the old tin roof.
    By clocks, calendars, nights, days

By fast, by slow, by high, by deep;
by sing, by dance, by laugh, by sleep;
by climb, by fall, by jump, by walk;
by chance, by breath, by cry, by talk;
by clocks, calendars, nights, days.
    By clocks, calendars, nights, days

Atua of Nowhere Zen

Elders photographed staring at gold-rush sun
could not see daylight through a Union Jack,
or rabbit after rabbit bolt from the gun.

Kids in cotton smocks made sing-song;
mustered for Anzac biscuits, gathering
blue-gum leaves to blow a cheery tune on.

Merino jumpers were strung along
the wee gully; with father out fencing,
a slip of a girl tackled the flock alone.

Hail ploughed its block of despond;
thickened a Captain Cooker's hairy back;
encased a sod hut; flattened a fern frond.

The far volcano's catapulted boulder
dropped from dug-up sky like a hot scone
to land smack on Lake Taupo's kisser.

Tuatara crawled to the swimming snow
of bridal-veil falls, that had such a glow
as worms had prophesied, under Waitomo;

but hiding out like a bush-ranger's grave is
the spot where all rain forest goes to rack,
and only the caterpillar remembers this.

The historic places turn towards a dream
while necklaces of votive whalebone, worn
by astronauts of inner space, gleam.

Clouds sail sweet bouffant flotillas;
possums stew; sheep cook by the book;
a godstick spells tales of grandmothers.

The tour guide buzzes, like a fly, stuck
in the marmalade of bitter autumn
varnishing all the hills of Nowhere Zen.

Colonial Pidgin

Sailing ships rose
to whale-road's wallow,
and the mollymawk
      flew high . . .
   coasting down to
grazing cloud,
catchment fern,
tide-lines.

Snarls of barbed wire
    rust beneath clay,
the colour of a put-out fire,
    awaiting a better day.

Fern sap bubbles gummy from ponga.
Sun burns hot tar scooped off the hard.
Dropping his clutch of mushroom caps,
a bewhiskered oldster staggers
    between used tea-cups,
    plates; rolling the makings
    and coughing catarrh,
    he steels himself,
as existence sharpens to a knife-point
    and — twists.

Erewhon Unearthed

Skies run, streaked bloody like fleeces shorn.
Strainers twang symphonies in milk and gold.

Empire Rose and *Sun Boy* sail on the tide.
Daisies nod from spring paddocks, stirred.

Tussock's sunbaked pelt jumps and rolls.
Sugar spoons rattle with tea-shop's prattle.

The moa's calcified rugby ball shines,
plucked from scrums of muddy leg-bones.

Hail pings grave bell-jars in sad chimes;
the snick of tiny hail counts baby teeth,

as tree stumps whiten along Dead Horse Row.
Corsets rip, stripped back to whalebone cages.

Found tremors unearth time's brass-bound capsule.
Wings glow amber inside kauri gum's weight.

Glass arcades surface from submarine depths.
Going for a skate, with beer belly bounce,

truckloads of grey silt are chucked up high.
Cashmere Hills cardigans, faded to pink,

shrink in the wash of a bushwacked laundry.
The smell of money leaves the oily rag,

tossed back and forth by whole-earth mechanics.
Coin's flipped downside promotes a fire sale.

Heretics get stuck in with a mixed hot grill.
Bats climb, freed by the great snail's betrayal.

Colonel Shag's cliff-face cormorants preen,
while zephyrs ride, teased by sailboard teens.

Sound and Fury

Not stony silence in Kiwi backblocks,
but quiet rustling of ferrets and stoats,
the blether of sheep, the blither of wind,
road gangs scraping shovels in two-four time.
Bang, bang of settlers throwing up a house;
diggers, back and forth, toss screwball yarns.
Stockwhips crack and bullockies curse;
a steam train crosses sixty-five bridges.
Old-guard swan-song, heehaw of Bonassus;
while Bob Semple crowed as he rode the land,
it seems he failed to catch the Royal Ear.
Magpies' quardle-oodle-ardle-wardle
heard as cat-bell and dog-whistle remix;
motorvating truck drivers ditto that uptick.
Bogans, cashed-up, await gentrification,
seeking a personal tutor in Enzed Lit.
Skim and Scam, borne by budget jet,
arrive from Greece to fleece supermarket flocks.
A crusader caped in Silver Fern flag
conjures Anzackery from an army surplus bag.
The gurgle of a pollie's liquored voice signs
uncashable cheques in front of cameras
with the silver plume of a heron feather.
White-gold pipelines chugging towards town,
irrigator stutter sucking the well-bore dry,
bring the sound and fury of moo-moo land,
Hear the hoofbeats of stampeding herds;
be last man standing in a rolling maul;
and from deep depression in the Tasman Sea,
be rescued by blood of the underdone lamb.

Oamaru Cavalcade

Who, beside the broken orders of architecture
dug from ochre and finessed for glory
as gargoyles and seraphim, carved buttery, creamy,
could hear the parade's steampunk fanfare,
against clouds' top hats of tantrum thunder, with dust
peppercorn-powdery on the masks of Donna Demente,
and on the skins of play-acting servants and swaggers,
strolling after penny-farthings under bunting,
after brewers' drays that bump over drains,
while Shakespearean princes look daggers
at villains staging hold-ups with cap-guns
stealing through cloisters and granary,
up on hind legs like ships' rats ashore,
as the periwigged brandish ear-trumpets rust-crusted,
from basket and limp balloon, bladdery,
draped on the back of a slow-moving truck,
in the general direction of bird-stuffers,
and sheepish gluttons for barbecued meat,
in muttonchop whiskers forming a ruck
to rip chops from the carcass of a sheep
lying in state on a bed of parsley
with cries of hip-hip-hooray?

Ears hung with marbled greenstone
bright as cut-open kiwifruit,
pantomime tohunga tear at tatau with whalebone,
while gutters brim,
and pedigreed pigs squeal — to wheel-beaten
eggwhites, to meringue interiors, to sugar tongs,
to jumble-sale cakes, to whitestone
church frontages — from a cage on a ute,

that sounds its horn the way whales mourn;
and tea-cups rattle spoons in smoky rooms,
where a chapter on wars is consulted in the book of hours,
amid storm-light, the horse trot of a cavalcade,
as churchwarden pipes are puffed
by surveyors of the soapsuds
which are travelling with the speed of a wet week,
over paddocks cobbled by wheat-straw,
and over the tops of autumn trees,
gold-leafed in rainway's door.

Provincial Champions

We upped stumps at greyed-out end of play,
tramped down Foxton Straights, gathered steam,
took toheroa without tears, made pāua eyes,
pulled rabbit after rabbit from the top paddock,
chucked an oval ball that carried team weight,
ran up a batch of scones, downed keg after keg,
feasted large on a barbecued beast's hind leg,
raised a pedestal to games of knucklebones;
so, mustered bluster of a thousand clichés,
travelled quiet through Southern Cross-lit night,
collected swamp donkeys out of fog's murk,
strangled their teats, made them squirt,
heard milky gurgles rise in steel silos,
and were home and hosed before dawn rose.

Watching the Detectives

Unnoticed, lie corpses of weasel and magpie;
the feral pig stinks, dressed in mould.
Something killed them, something old.
He punches, kicks, and swears awry
at wigging heads of rams,
batted back by bleating lung;
they bare a yellow fang, raise a cry,
in acrid tang of urine and dung.

A queue quibbles between tills;
the entrance to the tunnel's closed,
but this is no excuse for the mourners
to drop their casket and rush to the hills;
the hills will be a slog from the word go.

A profit and loss prophet leans at a drunken angle,
running off at the mouth in a jingle-jangle;
his drool's caught by the wind factor,
and spun out as a sun-struck web,
like the web a wasp is funnelled into,
where a tiny spider jiggles for joy,
running across the rigging to snare
with more threads the maddened creature.

Spring's stipple of pollen mantles the window,
a gentle detective dusting it for fingerprints,
in a motion soft as slow blowflies that spiral
out of bodies of dead rats on the compost.
Flies graze on cake; the wind murmurs.

There was a death, but now things grow;
voices writhe into life at the wake after the funeral.

Before Compulsory Drug-testing Begins

Purple tinctures to ease the intolerable,
sugar crystals to sweeten the detestable,
heavy veils to conceal the hideous —
on horseback they ride, morbidly virtuous,
smoking opium through days of mourning,
by turbulent waters when skies are raining.
From verandah to verandah, they gaze at the sea,
Victorians in dressing gowns drinking their tea.
With last gasp, the versifier clutches a quill;
uses kauri gum residue to seal the will.
There's borer in the floorboards, borer in the walls;
and a kiwi trussed in a bombazine bonnet,
dragging ripe tawa berries in its claws,
down in the basement, signed off on a sonnet.

Beacon

The glow-worm says, let there be light.
Axes bold as love strike for the heartwood.
The kauri table remembers the forest,
and the conch shell calls to the sea.
Through a candy shimmer the waves
on shore open their summer novels.
Crickets' midday curriculum goes scritch-scritch.
Kazoos, comb-and-paper, and harmonica
begin the bee and wasp summer orchestra.
An orchestration of herds, too, undulant
as tentacles and flowing like a lowing river.
Stones rattle backwards at Trotters Gorge.
Lake salmon leap in silver-blue plumage.
Four-wheel vortex, chipmunk techno, bleeps at sunset.
A possum growls, another howls, a third coughs.
Fugitive shadows steal across the moon.
Pebble-mouthed creeks lisp wicked to night stars.
Emerson's 'Bookbinder', cold as an eel's nose.

The Opening of Toi o Tāmaki Refurbished, Rugby World Cup, September 2011

Each crinkle of scoped sky's plunge to earth yawns.
The thousand distractions a mind is heir to, blink;
inmost heart's wellspring is stained with pollen,
or piss, as mountaineers pick their way up stairs
of villas down hillsides, churches raised on clouds;
every prospect pleases and only man is vile,
caught by revolving doors of Toi o Tāmaki:
crypts for agoraphobics, stuffed with art,
vampire grottos behind sheer glass on Albert Park,
as bumble-footed, wall-eyed ones with hands
that want to wander, but must not touch, join
squirmers, my-kid-could-do-thats, the head-cocked.
Crowd spins like a rugby ball, stops in a hurry:
messengers flying lights down Queen Street's gully.

Between Two Harbours

Portage Road stretches between two harbours.
You are here. Sun's on the face of the deep.
Small green volcanoes rise like tsunami waves.
Clouds darken, rain-slicked, and unreef.
A lizard ladders up a wall. A wing tip turns.
An ant strives along a concrete pavement.
Wind bounces through pinnacles of tall trees.

Dazzled traffic waits at lights in trapped shoals,
stopped by red beneath three-masted clouds
that pass fast as bows of racing schooners.
Windscreen wipers fend off rain-slick blur,
but it swims anyway in my green realm.
Showers skip or slide over hulls of cars.
Sea's an echo sounder for Auckland's shells.

Absolute abba abba, the sun, drowned
into this world, rose, daylight before dark,
to become a ship drawn by the grateful dead,
of whom … I swallow this bitter medicine.

Saltwater shawls fall. Tears, spray and foam
curl gold and grey to scud as veils of wet,
running down reflections in corroded chrome.
Wraiths I pursue till sightless with my heart.
Your spirit walked north across the brine —
so home the sailor, the airman home for tea.

With isthmus for compass, skies are clearing,
full-sail blue, like proud regatta clippers.
Dolphins breach in arabesques to tumble

through bubble towers lit up. Dungeon
torches burn with green flames at depth.
Aureoles crown absinthe's sorrow.
From seaweed tangles I woke this morning.

Flying boat engines chatter their reverie.
White terns are wind-swept in accelerando.
In slow formations of gulls that follow,
I trace your wake on echoes of the sea.

FIRE

Night Flight to San Francisco

Hello world, your newscasts stream
in hallucinogenic braids, as the cabin crew arms the doors.
There are channels showing charlatans stoking emotions;
blurs of fingers pointing in all directions;
the love-bombed expressions of refugees eating burritos.
Moneyed humans with bandoliers are still at large.
A fire scales walls, leaps hedge funds,
is given thrilling credence.
The whole plane's a clutch purse with a glitch;
and we tumble into our seats like loose coins,
as if riding a pandemic out of Guangdong
on three hundred thousand horses.
The obsolete Marxist locomotive of history
is shunted into a siding,
to be crushed for cyborg innards.
The tsunami of births retreats,
leaving the ground littered with twisted bodies.
Out of darkness, firefly squid rise to the surface.

Plucked from ocean's nether regions,
an afflatus of angels flickers in green flashes,
amid a hurly-burly of insurgent waves
in the Kermadec Trench, in the Fiji group.
A horseshoe magnet pulls us to the Equator,
where a hunting dragnet trawls.
Endocrine disruptor spreads through the wash,
the Pacific Garbage Patch.
To what resort do reef fish flitter?
Who hunkers over a slug
of therapeutic nihilism mixed with bitters
in front of the six o'clock news any more,

as the sheep looks east, the cow looks west,
and Muttnik's ashes orbit the carpark?
The masses are mechanically wending
between vending machines
in search of the god that failed.
The heat of an all-seeing invisible eye
is being cooled by extractor fans.
Backs of heads rise in rows like new planets.

This flight is non-stop:
a frigate bird in dimmed fulguration.
So the sleep of reason snores,
and the brain fears aneurism,
or a twenty-four hour power nap.
In the aisle queue, count your blessings,
past imperfect and future tense.
The tea-break urn overfloweth.
The writer squeezed up on a squashy banquette
is off-script, and fame looks away.
So to the celebrity crush of minuscule muesli cup,
greasy omelette, whipped creampuff cloud
laced with passionfruit pulp.
Maddening, like a flash-gun rewound,
the dazzle of the sun on your face.
Landing gear lowers its roller-skates,
high on fifty states of mind.
A funky video game crash-lands in a blinged-up city.
Screen-engrossed keyboardists
are tapping in their glass-sided turrets
the shape of cigarette packets.
The doors are disarmed;
there's a leaf in the beak of Noah's dove.
Jeeps approach, packed with life coaches.

Six Days as a Manhattan Island Castaway

In my hotel, the Jane, craning out the small window
of the stifling box they call a room, I'm a trapeze
artist let down from a jet plane into storied Gotham;
don't call it jet lag; call it Spiderman's vertigo.
On Jane Street, the gilded bellhops jump, slam-dunk,
and jive up steps away from winter, with baggage.
We're near Bleecker Street; it leads to Greenwich Village.
I'm one of the bards who bowled up in a yellow taxi;
we might have crash-landed on the Hudson and floated
to shore on airbags, invited to read Enzed poetry
here for Phantom Billstickers, at Saatchi and Saatchi.
The subway is a gritty, sulphurous, clanging disco,
with rail screech, fast footfalls and turnstiles a-go-go.
Homeless huddle around the walls just to kill time;
across grey knuckles, they catch and flick a dime;
armed response cops look busy chasing crime.
From steam laundry drizzle and infernal combust,
past shiny metal buckles, burnt smell of upper crust,
I weave streets, among bike couriers, hot dog vendors,
to pay respects at the space of the World Trade Center.
Gotham's air smokes like a Civil War tobacco plantation.
Commuters shuffle through low-roofed Penn Station.
Avenues are flooded with red, white and blue flags;
bodies in mittens, mufflers and hats resemble sandbags.
Periscopes of brick submarines peer at daylight gloom.
In cafés, each solitary is busy with a smartphone.
Down Broadway, buses roll silver and hiss to a stop,
as sleet slashes on railed parks, on brownstone blocks.
I'm an extra in *New York the Movie*'s crowd scenes:
its sass, its rap, its diner fug, its Times Square blare.
I climb with superhero traction to blinky-blink heights,

and from the Art Deco roof of Rockefeller's Center I drop,
to cross Central Park with its paths labyrinthine,
and tourist-gawk at squirrels, prowl cars, HBO crew.
The piano-black President's convoy is green-lit through
from the Lincoln Center, and wet skins of limos quiver,
idling outside Guggenheim's Gallery in gridlocked streams.
Gogglers throng Apple Store's translucent techno;
and Fifth Avenue deli-kings up the sales tempo,
to squelch of gumshoe and sprays from rubber wheels.
Strap-hangers ride the express, clinging to their iPods.
The train seems to swim through ferromagnetic clouds.
I surface next stop as if from beneath an ocean.
Neon's gutter flare-out crumples Valentine-red,
and there's more cold drizzle on the Lower East Side.
Rain beckons from the Bowery; steel grates squeal.
Outside a church some jesus freaks hum and talk;
one declaims Ezekiel, chapter four, verse three:
'It shall be a place for spreading nets into the sea.'
I open my umbrella struts to their full span.
The fabric bulges taut; then I start to walk.

Ode to Coffee

for Larry Matthews

Even from the first sip,
carousels of whirling cups start up,
and that rollercoaster loop-the-loop
Haunted Mansion fluttery bats feeling,
that Fun Mountain Climb blue ceiling sensation,
that whinny of hoof beats across the heart,
that giddy sugar-shock hit as neon flashes
and you float through hysteric glamour on the liquid mean.
So here's the thing, the molecular throw-down,
whether a skinny on a leash,
or a power mango latte in a grease-
trap, or a double-decaf with almonds to set
yourself up for a mega-mall go-around —
though light-years away from the caramel-
coloured hard-sell of industrial flavours and Planet
Heartburn's 'tree-fresh' o.j. —
whether black for the red-eye, the jet-lag,
black for the loved-up, black even unto those that gag
at bitter crystallisation of seething wells,
and each drop a silky piano note
steamed from the roasted bean,
cupped in cardboard, polystyrene,
painted glass, or hand-thrown ceramic,
and summoning up wavering syrups of Araby,
wraiths of Colombian mojo elixir,
haloes of Ethiopian mist, earth spices,
java jive, Papuan sing-sing,
or atomic Afro's joyous-bubbled woosh,
here's the thing: had you the ability

to read those grounds, you might see
that the concept, let this be
your commodity fetish,
has ever schemed
its slo-mo assumption
of your taste-buds,
even from the first sip.

Testament of Databody Dave

Hello, Databody Dave here — what am I but
a collection of information items subject to panoptic
tracking and Cloud control: the eternal sunshine
of the spotless mind? Am I interrogating the system,

or is the system interrogating me for a predictive
Wikipedia of the self? What I Know Is just a search
for a signal in the noise, joining the typing arms
race of eager communicators. Once were a nation

of conspicuously absent consumption, where everything
happened behind closed doors; now we've thrown the house wide
to open-plan indoor-outdoor flow, barbecue pits
and its own Facebook page, as doddery old

diddy men, knowing diddley-squat about anything
any more, join the young net surfers who only know
on a need to know basis, otherwise content to chew gum
and post skateboard near-misses, as their earbud iPod fizzes.

Facebook, what is that but electronic galley slaves
furiously pounding keyboards to row their boat forward,
making users strike-targets for predatory sales teams,
trapped in a status-sphere of cool apps and stale pap

as technocapitalism's endless ooh and aah soundtrack
forms an unbreakable compact to provide finer
and finer tweaking of social networking via avatars,
substitutes and personalised kilos of sugar?

Outpourings as unstoppable as the Huka Falls:
tiddlywinkers with tapered fingers twiddle
out texts and Twitter tweets, stripping a topic bare —
locusts moving on, having appropriated, eviscerated,

and marketed yesterday's news as a must-have,
must-see version of same old same old echo chambers
of like-minded sharers maintaining vigils of the vigilant
and threads of the dead on behalf of opinion research agencies.

They get up your nose with their fibre-optic hose,
their cold calls offering flim-flam to confuse.
You will know them by their rhubarb, rhubarb, rhubarb,
those gurus selling spiritual values in soluble capsule form

with talk of naked society, surveillance society,
franchise society, atomised society, sedated society,
but if you look round to blame someone, no-one's
there, just algorithms taking care of business.

Six billion's a crowd, but seven billion's crowd-sourcing,
with givers, takers, window-lickers in cyberspace,
and ambulance-chasers assembled in the distance,
as green actors attempt to offer some resistance

to an anarchic world of pass-the-parcel debt,
shadow banks, vulture capitalists, Milton Friedman,
the glub-glub of boat people pushed under by boat
shoes of the best-performing banksters in Oz.

I'm so over it, the over-easy, over-familiar,
over-consumed, slack-jawed, over-done, over-run-
by-cruise-ship, big-bang boomer mentality:
all one heaving packing case of banjaxed bollocks.

Fatigued hipster seeks hipster replacement therapy:
escape from the knowing winking calculating flattery;
the quantitative easing for the squee and the twee;
yet another colloquy of sippers and garglers

fumigating their bridgework with finest pinot noir,
furtively consulting phones for inflammatory spam
in the mirrorball gleams of a casino beano,
while battlers grope for change on their knees outside.

I'm drinking decaf in the global warming.
I'm hunched over a gasper in the global aging.
I'm perched on a push-bike in high-visibility vest,
and updating my status: @ hand-jiving
high-fiving, bumping-booty, total-retro frug-fest.

New Zild Book Awards Considered as a Five-Horse Race

They're off and racing now, a boxed set
at first, away fairly well down the straight.
And it's open slather, as the front three break
loose from Holus Bolus and Hoi Polloi,
already struggling to keep up
with the favourites. Giddy Goat's
book of poetry is parked on the outside,
as Chomping Chum's novel leads,
followed by How's Yer Father's
biography. Yes, Chomping Chum's
the leader now, by a length from Holus Bolus
and the rest … here comes Chomping Chum,
coming home great guns. No, Giddy Goat's
scampered clear, followed by How's Yer Father.
Giddy Goat and How's Yer Father neck and neck,
but wait it's Chomping Chum through the middle,
scattering the dirt, getting his head just past the post,
by a nostril, by a toothbite. Just pips How's Yer Father
being gored by Giddy Goat, Chomping Chum is champion!

The Wisdom of Crowds

World's confetti of scratch and sniff cards;
but too many free gifts and we might lose
our bearings: our search engine of memory
choked with lava flows from the centre
of the planet; so we breathe out fumes,
and move as one through a trance of days,
spinning our yarn so it stays spun,
begun as we mean to go on forever, though
those of the dead who can be made to speak
don't want to return, prefer where they are.

Yet how beset we seem by verbal muzak,
swapping confidences, the pull of gravity's
emotion sculpted to a smile; your name here.
Please hold, your call is important to us,
they say; still those waiting room moments
drip slow as hot wax from votive candles.
We orbit the sun and audit the sun,
to unhinge the doors of perception,
though there is nowhere to go but indoors,
ghost forms jiving inside our jazz tongue.

How to make good on careless promises,
those chance remarks, these flights of fancy?
For we cling to one another's coat-tails
so as to soar to the empyrean
on our slightly different frequencies,
as errors amplify that creep us out
with their fidelity, their nuances that
wobble like jelly, a rippling quake
to register our silence, the brief pause
before heroic moment's vox humana roars.

Browser

Drunk on ink,
the bookworm bores
through printed words to paper cores,
then lies down in darkness,
munching through a library.

My history is a webbed nightmare
from which I am trying to awake,
the viscosity of black ink
now a billion times told uglier
and more stupidly brutal,
amid pulsing digits,
like a witchcraft fable
of sticky burning pitchblende.

One another in one another's arms.
Alphabets, bed-bound, listen
to dying songs of the dead and gone,
who no longer have moral qualms
about the dope with the mostest,
the gene unseen,
the nuclear test, the hypothalamus test,
the rabbit hiding in the hat,
the loss of loss.

And everything else
is the purest kind of blue, tried and true,
Lawrence of Arabia blue,
but with an abbatoir chill.

Is This You?

Clinch, hug, break, smile, raise your hands together.
Fist bump and high five are preferred to middle finger,
but no-one watches the humdinger,
so you move fast and break things,
being fake-happy, and living at
some time in the mid-Pliocene era,
when the world was a whole lot warmer.
So what if the clinks of dollars ring true —
the rest is tiddlywinks,
and you get no change from nineteen ninety-nine.
Is this you?
The boomtown bombast is moving your way,
to bring winking bracelets,
the feel of yesterday on your skin —
that's the you that's trying to catch
the colour of each season,
the taste of the morning,
the noise of the evening,
the crush of happy hour.
All containers are overboard,
and you're my shipwreck of the dinner set,
on the rocks with a twist of lime.
I got you, but as tunnel vision.
I got the herky-jerky jump-cut you,
The Nouvelle Vague in vogue you,
but count on it —
you will eventually wave and waver
and rise in stardust, whistling,
to where some brand-name bling-meister twinkles.
Dinosaurs will be doing lunch.
That will be something, something to tell your children.

Freedom Songs of the Vietcong

John Doe spoke from our back porch in sixty-six,
in bad tones, to channel Victor Hugo at fever pitch.
'I may not make old bones,' said he —
and the Eight Immortals were crossing the sea —
'but I know that wherever I may roam' —
and he cupped his hands like a megaphone,
his face desolate, his tears sprung on cue —
'I'll seek the Gate of Luminous Virtue.'

A Shankar raga spun on the stereo,
I see him there still, though it was years ago,
picked out in darkness by fluoroglare,
a wide-eyed Polaroid with shaggy hair,
teeth tubes humming like a tuning fork,
tripping on a tab of Windowpane's torque,
Over Mekong's Delta droned bomber planes,
black smoke from rice paddies reflected flames.

Dust devils gathered in Auckland's summers,
to the clang-clang of Thirteenth Floor Elevators,
Moby Grape acid, Strawberry Alarm Clock,
groovy vinyl go-go boots on the hop.
Ho Chi Minh's trail of gardens lay concealed,
filaments of sticky silkworms unreeled,
dragon clouds grew from a napalmed bodhi tree,
newsreels showed monks burning for liberty,
as John Doe undid the name tag from his big toe,
and danced to 'Barbara Ann' in our family bungalow.

Exquisite Corpse

… drive thy camels speedily in their direction …
— MOHYUDDIN IBN 'ARABI

The exquisite corpse of the dreaming poet
is shipped to France in a wooden kimono
partitioned with dishdasha fabric, with juju,
with hoodoo, with flavour of red cordial
than which no hubble-bubble could be sweeter.
Ah, quill-sharpener! Spear carrier! Delivering
a beautiful javelin throw through the chest,
odours of hair products wafting in your yard,
tinfoil on the windows, so that smackdown
at grey paint-stripper dawn for Tourette's
syndrome charmers, throats thick with glitter
after all those tennis court oaths, might be
a little less scrapmetal, more a jangled fanatical
pilgrimage to junkyards of tossed glow-
stick lyricism and trickled poteen elixirs.

Remember Hitachi, Yamaha, Sony, Suzuki;
the abracadabra of authentic Somali pirates;
sips of sherbert in recesses of a Dubai souk
that shields a sheik away from blowtorch
breath of ships of the desert; and din of
Turkmenistan carpet vendors in Ashgabat
bazaar; throat singers' melismas in Ulan
Bator; the silent obelisks of Axum;
prophetic seal meat in Nuuk; the smile ripe
as Papeete mangos on a street in Linwood?

These shredding 1001 dreams you must have
before you wake tell you the poem is all; as
by a vortex, everything's engulfed by the poem,
until in and of each thing — in time, in time —
clarinet, perfume bottle, yacht, the tangerine
you squeeze, how you're put on hold, digital
smears across the accused, ways to stay alive,
to scat or jive, speak in celestial tongues, or
run off at the mouth, is just word jazz, right?
Oh, syncopate, you skid row skidders, you
stumblebums, you down-and-out park bench
beat poets on easy street, thinking of ways
to profit from an end-of-lifetime clearance.

Don't be a chumposaurus, busting your chops;
be a stand-up guy in primeval swampland,
prime resident at that aforementioned dawn,
the last man standing in a line-up for the firing
squad, who suddenly finds he is a jumbotron
clown in a sentence queuing at a full stop,
watching a little guy called Elf, caught on a shelf,
waving a pitchfork and a warm bottle of tequila.

You want a hex with that mojo, or a symphony
of self-assembling furniture?

I bask in the glow of your burning cookbooks.

The brainwaves of your thought-crime capsize
my oil tanker complex.

What's your god? Get it straight. Your eyes
interact with the blur of seek and destroy.

Your message to calm a tuning fork,
your memory of loyalty to graffiti,
your half-baked sneakers —

pull the pin on bubblegum.

Night Shades

They turn, and you see a tip of flame
reflected from the lighter up close,
each eye bracketed by a frame,
face pinned in place by shades,
little boxes to house the gaze —
walled-in space, viewless vision.
They might punch your lights out.
Future's in shades, black on black,
a cosmic zenith of rock star glitz,
or else zilch of shadowed tribunals,
funerals for the null and void,
cameras for denizens in zoos.

They turn, so you see a tip of flame
reflected from the lighter up close,
and caught light orbits each frame,
as if the opaque lenses are a question,
or a questioner inside the haze
of the question posed by that razor
glitter of obsidian, its closure
and erasure. Eye seeking eye —
a goo-goo eye, a terror eye,
a zero eye, a tranced eye,
a pinned eye, a wheeling eye,
the blank eyeless staring abyss.

Superyacht

I

A climbing rope is vaporising into smoke;
it is the benchmark of the hangman's noose.
A shiny medal is being pinned to a breastbone.
Rippling torsos arrive, garlanded with tripe;
slot-machine heads gobble coins.
Something ticks in hollow eyes of clock-faces.
Skeletal race-horses clack the track.
Who waits in trench-coat and a written-off suit?
She's shaking hips and tits, hair woven into snakes.
He's pegging out the nappies, as scrap-iron thorns
catch plastic bags blossoming in the wind.
Let us track down and excavate the dream,
in breathless anticipation of pepper spray.
Let us search for the face beneath the scream,
knowing there will be no more quiche and blue jeans today.
Let us write the alphabet in mirage on mirage;
then let us leave this huge sea inlet before ice encroaches.
More lands will appear on a daily basis in maps.
The only cosmonaut left above will ease up on steroids.
Weather guys will have tracked a cream mausoleum
of marbled cloudscapes descended from God's big toe.
The syndrome will declare itself sick, and close the book.
The hum of the air-conditioning will lull you all night.

II

The shape of a pop-up toaster has sailed from port.
The whisper of a cue word has caressed you
in a closed circuit of rooms.
The sun-cured businessman moves to left-over mugs;
who was it who tweaked his cheek,

scales of justice stashed in the back pocket?
In the slow burn down to midnight's gunshots,
that medallion proud on the battlefield of his chest,
he proves himself more deadly than the rest.
Squashed under the tattooed thumb,
he presses the flesh in a crush bar of well-wishers
and touchers, disappearing into the whirlpool,
smooth as a machine-gunner, mowing down the crowd.
Can gold-braided brigadiers find such motivation?
There is a stench from the dark grave of the mouth.
Tongues snake from throats, from death on the never-never.
Fingers are gouging, pushing, punishing;
squid-like hands grip their machinery.
That defence mechanism sounds out of line.
These savage sheep are out of time.
An auto-destruct button is gravely worn.
A pedigree diploma is grimly torn.
Terrible tales of guitar abuse go around.
Press gangs rove between classified columns,
jerky as glove puppets righting wrong.
Twitching switchblades catch evening light,
and turn into sun-reflecting windscreens.
Salty tars hold the mooring ropes of a superyacht.
Soda siphons are foaming.

Threads

Lasers comb through threads wide as human hair;
servers host cells that house the cloud that cares;
cross-legged on the cloud repose trillionaires.
Firms arise, merge, expand, and disappear;
only to reverse-engineer the next tax year.
White collar, steel collar, no collar worker:
each becomes an online multi-game player.
Chalk guidelines down the suit of a banker
act as a standard minute value reminder
of the fashion distress of child labour,
and force the ethical hiccups of a hipster,
who wears sandblasted jeans lifted from the sewing floor,
as threads of vapour traced by nails of a raptor
are pressed and crushed inside a screen of glitter.

The Death of Gaddafi

We perch in our eyries looking on,
ripened and rotting,
some with a migraine
seething like maggots in the brain,
others with thoughts like abscesses pus-filled,
that maybe this is art hanging from a gibbet,
castrated by carnivorous birds,
or bloody as a movie's bullet ballet,
while voices of the great unwashed
rise to vapour trails,
and junoesque jezebels —
jacuzzi jazz babies clad
in a job-lot of global oddments — sling Kalashnikovs
to jab at compulsive tourists in arresting scenes,
and at those souvenir hunters who reminisce
through the twentieth century's auction rooms
with throat-clutching sentiment.

So he crept doubtful and twitching
down the dark interstices of pipes,
emerging between the grout and nubble,
where the hissing hesitancy of anticipation alarmed him,
and he collapsed in a nearby drain
where everything was kind of run-down
and second-rate, yet where also something
had teasingly begun to take shape,
a mirage of dust and shadows,
spelling the living end,
and smelling of petroleum as sun-up arrived
with the whomp whomp of rockets.

So tank salvoes wreck chrome logos,
where flashpoints flare, sunguns glare
and camera lenses blur the air —
thus the naked capitalist
with his cheesy soaps, his reversible bandannas,
his gold-plated pistol, does not, after all,
glide into the witness protection programme
with a sneer, but dies in a waking nightmare.

Glory be to rogue states and stateless rogues,
the convoys of exiles at home nowhere,
and driving from country to country,
as from their keys dangle shrunken heads —
so the story is told by his and hers newsreaders
who make a toothsome twosome,
and told by clique versus claque versus cabal,
and told by fame-machine journos phoning in the performance,
in anonymous international airport idiom
from non-publicity-shy-trouble-spots,
which are in a steady state of surface tension,
a steady state of glory be, glory be,
that serves as entertainment for the grounded
waiting by the conveyor belts for their ship to come in.

The neon tigers of the new democracy
splish-splash through blood money;
abetted by a smarmy army of media savants
in a sticky part of the globe leaking oil,
with all the moral cachet of a shampoo sachet.

So here's to a non-recognition of the nameless,
to the permanent maladjustment
that will never reanimate the depersonalised,

as the mob bolts, parcelling out angst,
frenetic plastic, bales of cash, bank bonfires.
His death is an opera, a narcosis, a new religion
to inflame the veins
and become lightning flashes
deep inside the brainstorms of his tribe.
His fluff has been napalmed off
and fed to chimneys, to smokestacks of rumour mills,
by a crowd of animated gargoyles
coming off a hit, a fix;
and scunge has left its high tide mark on him,
as if he had been doped to his dead eyeballs,
to the golden bullet points
of his stabbed corpse presentation,
the four hundred thousand blows of ill-feeling
addressed to his legacy;
for democracy is the burn-off of body fat,
democracy is a Coke robot on every street corner,
democracy is the look of the outlaw
on the face of the consumer,
and the sound of branded chains talking crappuccino,
for these are the last days of general rhetoric,
before the platforms are vacated,
and the knowing bodies buried
under the jargon of obsolescence,
leaving only a fragrance of sweatshop.

Your Call May Be Recorded

To pill-pop's compulsory, but we're forbidden smokes.
Blokes weep, drunk on sunset cocktails in false dawn colours.
Girls splurge, then purge, maxed-out by steals of the year.
We're vajazzled, bedazzled; overshare with junk food.
Internauts, we're backlit by burn-offs of hair-care product.
We wave status weapon handbags that spill must-haves.
Our starter kits of loyalty cards are swallowed, screwed
up after three goes of miscues, a failure to buy.
Fluoro blobs of orange vests strain our optic nerves.
Maimed by radiation cures, we walk zoo corridors
seeking the skill-sets of a chimpanzees' tea-party;
and in silence interrupted by literary lions' proud roars,
we launch for cyberspace before denial of service.

The Age of Terror

'If there's one person they're going after and there's 34 other people in the building,
35 people are going to die.'

Praise be to internet, now my mind is a search engine:
a web-headed weave around humanity
every which way that babbles of conformity,
and of dissenters in each departure lounge.
Can you step in the same data stream twice?
Satellites will eavesdrop on your advice.
The red dots dance their moody existence,
chased by cameras trained to turn,
and stealth drones hang in the listless air
listening for heartbeats that say human,
only to hear low hums of server farms,
and the hollow squalls of car alarms;
or is it feedback of prophets alarmed,
walking backwards on peacetime manouevres
and humming under flags of convenience,
seen through Google Glass smoked darkly?
But I don't watch enough TV to know,
though Earth's artificial networks grow
to encrypted purpose, so robotic
before screens on-line that fingers data-mine,
putting it down in writing, in lightning;
and then they fold the known universe
into a parallel universe, time out of mind
and back as the peacock's scream
vaults the dream to plume the trees with flame,
while an announcer's toothy grin begs
mediocrity's intense inane: that smile spreads
its chemical haze over Iraq on a rack.

There are unknown knowns, and then there are the drones.
The redacted cellphone's pixels blink at code black:
you all look alike to me; you fit the description.
We have your signature; you're in our sights.
You are what's cooking on the Cooking Channel,
being waterboarded in sync to the noise
of absolute zero, as if you were Batman
caught in the radar of his own making,
or Gulliver taken in by the Houyhnhnns,
their neighbourly neighing. So the riot
of gardenias in Pandemonium blazes,
and hearts wilt before tomorrow's sorrow,
and the age of terror is without error.

Where Gods Live

The funambulist walks a tightrope of signs,
above all the lands sewn with landmines.
Icarus sails towards reckoning's horizon.

'Have a good war,' shouts Juno, 'you and your kind,'
to raw, sugar-powered overeaters anon,
while body liberation becomes a bind,
sold in squiggles and oodles of blather
as an outsourced empty-of-content brand
to wilful coalitions of the duped, who're
subject to weepings at detox sessions
by an alchemy of glut, of insectoid mass.

Saturn's men abseil from amen corner,
from bully pulpits, through the hole in the wall
that leads to banks of state: banks, those false
teeth sunk foundering on pulp complexes
of plutocrats paying it forward as bonuses,
as haircuts by children, as dead cat bounce.

Vulcan vanishes from the funeral process,
to float on waves that flood factories, where souls
grind up salvation that explodes in sparkles,
lighting cities, whose glands are tumours
on top of non-stop gigantic growth spurts.
Maddened seas bow to lunar attractions,
and deadly virtues snake through cyberswamps.

Aphrodite comes down off her high horse,
named Umbrageous Pulchritude, of course,
to turn into a contractual obligation skinny,

pinging gold on the beauty meter, though her
Echo's out-of-synch with the in-crowd as ever.

The lone eye of Cyclops blazes, a blue planet
on fire; watch his shanghaied stone head,
for, armless, it will body forth and re-arm.

Stop your dizzy music, Mars, in galaxies,
stop, amid caliphates and golgothas of skulls,
your empires of burst sputniks, shark culls.
The Statue of Liberty is in a bodybag.
Her pollution suit sings the rag mama rag —
the depleted uranium song, the unobtainium song.

Neptune's a whistleblower obliterated
by oil slicks that saturate the internet.
Rogue brokers ride each turbo-market.
Psychotherapists stay hotwired to debt.
We ascend where gods live, as dog days blend
and universal heat death waits out the End.

NOTES

Acknowledgements are due to the following publications where some of these poems first appeared: *Blackmail Press, Beyond the Scene, Broadsheet: New New Zealand Poetry, Catalyst, Grumpy Old Men, Hue & Cry, Ika, JAAM, Otago Daily Times, Phantom Billstickers,* the *Press, Starch: A New Zealand Literary Journal, Takahe, Trout.*

The poem 'Orogenesis' featured in a craft collaboration with jeweller Anna Claire Thompson as part of *A New Line: 8 jewellers 8 poets*, an event at the Otago Museum for the Caselberg Trust in 2010.

'Lighting Up in a Singer Vogue' was inspired by the art and artistry of Alistair Galbraith; 'River' is dedicated to Mahinārangi Tocker, whom I met at the *Baxter* concerts organised by Charlotte Yates; 'Ode to Coffee' was originally commissioned by Larry Matthews for an art exhibition in his home, and is dedicated to him. 'Between Two Harbours' is a poem written for my father, who died just before Labour Weekend in 2013.

I am grateful to Ursula Bethell Residency at the University of Canterbury during the second half of 2012, and to the University of Otago Wallace Residency at The Pah Homestead in Auckland in 2013, both of which allowed me the time and opportunity to develop and finalise this collection of poems.

I'd also like to thank Terence Rissetto, Fieke Neuman and Emma Neale for generous help, insightful feedback and valuable suggestions; and Fiona Moffat and Rachel Scott for design advice and editorial input. Special thanks to my brother Tonu Shane Eggleton for carving and printing the six woodblock images that link together *The Conch Trumpet*.